Finding Our Way Home

Messages, Stories and Poetry

Finding Our Way Home

Messages, Stories and Poetry

Any Inquiries contact:

cheryl.hiller@yahoo.com

Some of the poems in this collection first appeared in

Cosmic Civilization: E-Zine Vol.3; We Are One, Follow the

White Rabbit, Know Your Way, and Life: Shared thru Poetry

chapbooks; and on facebook.

Cover credit, photo taken by Kathy Nemeth-Serrano, 2023.

Cover design by Catherine Preus, 2023.

First edition.

Published by Four Wild Geese Design, Mount Shasta, California 96067

ISBN 979-8-9892496-1-9

Preface

What does Finding Your Way Home mean?

This can mean many things on different levels; safety, comfort, security on a very human level--

There is a saying "Home is Where the Heart Is". My home is a sanctuary, sacred–-Its where I connect to my ancestors, guides and family.

What examples in nature do we have of coming home? Certain fish and mammals, such as salmon and whales return to their birth place to spawn or breed.

In their later years of life, many humans return to their birthplace on Earth.

What about our origin in the cosmos? When we die and leave this human existence, do we return 'home'? Can we make this trip without leaving our Earthly body?

Return to Source.

Become Whole.

"When the Soul integrates old parts of its self, it simultaneously integrates with its human self."--Orasin Orasin

We 'return' home when we integrate all parts of ourselves.

"We are slowed down sound and light waves, a walking bundle of frequencies turned into the music of the cosmos, we are souls dressed up in sacred biochemical garments, and our bodies are the instruments through which our souls play their music."----Einstein

Contents

Reality by Cheryl

Handle each situation with finesse--

Trust that wisdom will guide you

Enter new territory with awe.

Expansion requires patience.

Your victory will be epic.

We'll all be the winners.

Your actions are your reality.

Advanced Directive by Darrel Johannes

Ask spirit what---
that is for you and
then, for the world at Large.

No bigger thrill and satisfaction exists,
in being human, as an assignment
that transcends time and space--

An assignment that actually mends
the fabric of the Universe---
We are it, my friends!

I think the reason I do not seem,
to be getting answers or messages
from the Great Beyond---this time in Shasta--
is because the Great Beyond is actually me, now.

There is no distinction--no me and them,
or here and there.
My thoughts may very well be--
their thoughts.
My vision, their vision.

I feel so strongly, that right now, right here---
we need every single willing soul on board
for the Shift.
Every single one of us will be given all we need
to transform darkness to light,
fear into love and
hate into mercy.

No Bigger thrill in humanity exists
than
becoming a peace maker---
first a peace maker internally,
then,
of course
an agent for the divine.
The Advanced Directive.

The Shift by Jennifer H.

The people who are using their energy--
Inappropriately

--as they learn to love themselves

--they are the ones who will shift the world

The countless acts of self love
is what will bring the new world
into Reality.

Happy Prophecy by Darrel Johannes

I woke up at 2:30 am in grief--
20 year history, here at Shasta.
"I was so much older then--
I'm younger than that now."

Key words--
Let and May, both,
indications that something is trying to come through.
It does not originate with me,
and not by my effort.

Its all about allowing.

Let the spirit lead the way,
so not to fall and fail.

May the Holy Face strengthen your faith,
warmth will create an atmosphere for you.

Let heaven reign in your home, and
blessings will be over the edge.

May the angels of heaven guard you, and
the stars burn for you.

Let the temple of the soul be warm,
there will be no sadness in it.

Let peace of mind come, and
let goodness live in your heart.

Happy Prophecy to All of You.

"I set before you Blessing and Cursing,
Life and Death, therefore
choose life that you and your
descendants may live."

I hope you dance
by A'Marie B. Thomas-Brown

I hope you take the time to remember
That the greatness you seek, you are
That in your becoming
That which you seek
You already are
Changing
Like the seasonal metamorphos's
Summer to Autumn
Autumn to Spring
To Winter in our knowing
Creating anew
That which innately is you

In the choosing of a shoe
The carving of a pumpkin
In the company of those
Who fill you to overflowing
Fellow sojourners, sisters, friends
Mothering, Fathering, spiritual kin
The flow of the ocean
The swell of the breeze
UndUlating with passion
In every life streamed

A force to be reckoned with
A dance
A harmony
Melodically sanctioned
Upon every street
Within every thought
Upon every feeling
Breathing with purpose
A most humbled beginning
And ending
And beginning

Choices and options
Decisions and chance
I hope when given the opportunity to
You dance, dance, dance
5

Messages by Le'Vell Zimmerman

#1

You feed what you fight.

Resistance to something is but a form of providing
energy to whatever you are resisting.

As the Creator your focus is always creating more
of whatever you are focusing on and never destroying it,
where the hologram does not acknowledge your preferences.

Only what you are emotional about.

For example; whatever you are passionately angry about is
what you are passionately creating more of via your own intense
emotions.

E/motion= Energy in motion

#333

#2

Whatever programs of limitation you accept about life,
you crystallize and subconsciously look for evidence
of them being true.

This is an activity of the Ego Mind identity, where it
desires
to "be right" at all cost.....

Even if it's not.

Even if it's harmful to you.

It's about being right with the Ego Mind.

This mental voice is self destructive.

The more stillness you practice, the more you
sense the guidance of your true self within the
Heart Space.

#333

#3

The Ego Mind identity serves a purpose beloved.

No, your healing is not about discarding the Mind,
but working with it as a tool of the Heart Space.

Your healing is in acknowledging it's not the core
of who you are, where you are not the "voice in your head".

(It's a tool of the Heart Space in making logical decisions
within the physical illusion you created from within the
Heart Space before entering the physical form.)

Love is beyond "logic", however logic is an aspect of the
limitations of the dualistic environment as a tool of your
evolution.

Once again, the Ego mind is a "tool", and not the foundation
of who you are as Infinite Intelligence.

#333

#4

Chasing outer attention is an act of those stuck within the
illusion.

This is not a "campaign" to sell the idea of healing beloved.

All must walk their own path, where respecting the free will
of others is reflective of your capacity of maturity as a soul.

This is not about them, but about you beloved.

Once again, this is a hologram having its foundation within
you.
7

Inside, then outside.

As you change, the world you observe will.

#StayRoyal

#5

This is not a "popularity contest" beloved.

Being dependent on external validation and acceptance from the outside is not sustainable, and makes you susceptible to emotional manipulation, where most unawakened souls are currently enslaved to the approval of others.

Similar to "a dog chasing it's own tail", seeking the approval of others is an endless cycle that remains self destructive.

This is about your capacity of self acceptance.

To Love yourself is to Love God.

The more you accept yourself, the more you accept all reflections "unconditionally".

Self Love is the foundation of all Love.

The choice is yours to heal beloved.

#333

#6

The greater your capacity to forgive and accept yourself, the more you have the capacity to pardon others.

All are doing the absolute best that they can beloved.

Including yourself.

Unconditional Love is the truth of who you are as the Creator.

Your spiritual maturity is reflective in your capacity of forgiveness.

8

Start with yourself.

Masters wear crowns.

Heal beloved.

#7

Acceptance is a demonstration of your omnipotence beloved.

This is your design, where everything is truly happening "for you".

Truly awakened souls are not giving energy to the projection of protection.

You can trust yourself.

There is only God.

This is your story.

When you change, the hologram will change.

You first.

#333

The Higher the Fewer
by Cheryl

The higher---
the fewer!

The higher the climb---
the fewer that make it.

The fewer
the greater
achievement.

When we go high enough---
we will escape
this roller coaster.

Critical Mass of Love
by Cheryl

Love is the way home.
--Go thru the Heart Portal.

4giveness is the way home,
--take the higher heart road.

Allowing keeps you there.

Children Within ~
by Mercy Hawkwomyn

One of my child selves hides under the pews of a comforting ancient church of beautiful architecture, with statues of Yeshua, the Mary's & grandmother St Anne for company.

Another child self of mine seeks solace in a tree house, in the woods by a lovely creek bordering a luscious green meadow with a vibrantly mature oak tree from which a wooden swing seat is fashioned.

Yet another youth self lingers in a well appointed artistically structured library with spiraling stairs to secret books on the top shelves. There are wooden tables with glowing lamps. Of course, a comfy velvet couch as well.

There is also a young self within that finds herself in a mystical dance space with wooden floor & mirrors. It has large windows over looking an intriguing garden; where another youth aspect of mine takes refuge among delightful flowers, herbs & fountains, resplendent with fruit trees.

I am retrieving my child selves from being hidden so that they may integrate feeling welcomed & as safe as currently possible with my adult self.

My mature Self, who has accumulated necessary wisdom & survival understanding, can guide my younger selves with perspective on navigating this current cultural predicament; to find beauty in moments of immersion with the natural world, in true Human Nature & the depth of Love mirrored within from Spirit Realm.

In this way the shock of myriad trauma experiences are cushioned with inner Knowing revelations; melting frozen & flight tendencies. Scattered frights, comforted & subdued with tender patient care.

I regain wholeness. A little here & more there , throughout the course of time. I become the Mother Hen collecting her chicks who have scampered away in duress ~

The extreme pain of severe loss carves caves for solace in the Soul.

~ From There to Here

Samuel, a very small fish by Shambala

Samuel was a small fish in the big sea, but he could swim deep, deep, deep. And he swam so free. His eyes on either side were open so wide to take in all that he did survey. Samuel was amazed at all the different life forms in the sea, he loved seeing the jellyfish like ballerinas moving effortlessly. He was afraid that a big fish that might eat him so he would hide in little crevices of beautiful colored coral and shells. But what Samuel loved most of all the mermaids. And though they were rare, he knew one lair where they did live. He would go just at a distance not to let them know and he would watch how they brushed their hair and giggled amongst themselves and had these objects that they looked into to see themselves with. He was fascinated and when they would sing his whole body would ring.

Well, one day Samuel was swimming in the sea and a bigger fish got him. But it was not as he thought it would be, when the fish swallowed him, he dissolved. He fe t he was now part of the fish looking through its eyes, observing all the sea. But it was still Samuel, watching, learning, and enjoying the swim.

Ahhh, this fish was a Dolph n, a mammal fish you see that had eaten Samuel as he swam. While the Dolphin rose to the surface so fast, it exhilarated Samuel, as it would leap. Oh, the Sun was a new thing to Samuel. He loved it when the Dolphin would leap and spin and oh the warm rays of the Sun touching his body, glistening on his own skin. And fell into the water, again and again. Oh such fun to be the Dolphin, don't you know. The dolphins swam the great sea in groups. So close, in higher mind communicating all the time as they grazed each others bodies playfully. This was also new for Samuel, singing, talking and making love. Celebrating Life, jumping into the sky and Sun. Oh, what fun! This was awesome! This was great! Samuel loved swimming in waves and curves and straights. And, by the seashore where he leaped and surfed he saw creatures now. They walked it seemed, standing upright, the opposite of him, in their being. How weird they looked and multi-color too. Samuel loved jumping near the shore to see this thing so new. Oh my goodness, what a world in which he was! The sea and air and Sun. One day Samuel was swimming with his pod, leaping up and down. But this time when he leaped, there was no Sun. There was water falling from the sky, as far as he could see, little drops. Each splash made a note, thrilling his every cell. What a delight, as he twisted and turned to learn. Yes, Samuel did flow with it all, letting go. What a wonder, being a dolphin in the sea. One day, the sharks came, but his dolphin friends came and chased them away! Ahhh, being in a group had its way.

Oh, they swam the sea, shores and deep, living life in joy and ecstasy. Samuel wanted to share this joy with all he could see. He tried to sing it. He tried to let them know of Love To Be...

13

Marine World
by Jan Dorrell

An enormous bounty of life, plants and animals
An escape, much needed.

Early admission
Sense of entitlement for privileged access

Smell of onions for hand feeding giraffes.
Children recoiling as thin, long, black tongues
Attempt to retrieve this treat.

Background of loud, impatient roars of giant Bengal tigers.
Monkeys alerting trainers to serve them long awaited breakfast
Using shrill, persistent chirping
At a volume best heard from a distance.

Flocks of colorful red, blue, green, yellow and orange lorikeets,
Perching on the excited hands of children
Partaking of a meal of seeds and fruits.

Lush green vegetation
Home to the vibrant, iridescent pink flamingos.

Children with tattered sketch books
Attempting to capture a personal interactive moment
In this enchanting setting.

Cheering crowds for the deafening,
anxiety provoking
Speed boat demonstration.

Viewing Orca whales creating loops of boring circles
In their too small, cramped, unnatural tank

Is there a plea in their vacant eyes to be freed?
I can hear their hollow wails at night from my home across town.
Is their woeful song reaching out for a receptive, caring ear?

A bounty of life, plants and animals.
An escape much needed.

The Full Picture
by Cheryl

We are like splashes of water,
mist off a stream---
Bouncing on the rocks,
rising in the light of the sun
to shine and sparkle,
only to fall back into the creek
and flow down with the rest.

When we become our purpose---
we rise and shine.
Become a prism---
that catches the light
breaking it open, into
the Rainbow spectrum,
Becoming the Full Picture.

Grave Gambit
by Cheryl

We are being assaulted on every side---
join this, come to this,
Up and down

Danger, danger Will Roger--
What does your internal compass say?
Follow that.

Win some--or learn some,
the voice in my head
has been pretty loud lately---
please--Turn it down--
just a little.

Secret Garden by Cheryl

In Oz,
Dorothy
was looking for a way back home---

A spell, talisman, or the wizard.
What did she learn
on her journey?

The wizard could not
give her
what she already had.

Don't Forget
the ancient magic---
We all carry.

You take your wand
where ever you go.

We each have
a Secret Garden---

There, we can
Access our hidden magic.

Hear the elemental song.
Meet with fairies and pixies.
Sit in circle with Sasquatch.
Listen to the flowers.

The shine of a sparkling creek---
carries the wisdom of the ages.

Our guides
        direct our path
        and protect us along our way.
In my garden
        the Unicorns stand guard---
        only the pure of heart may enter.
We all have a guardian angel---
Fairy
Unicorn

Dragon
Crystal
Tree or
Crow,
as unique as we are.

Like the fireflies
they offer light---
Serve as guideposts along the way.

Dorothy
went on a journey
to learn about magic.
Find her way home.
By helping others
she found her way.

This path
Elusive
Can not be forced.
Can not be captured, bottled or sold.
You can find it---
In the wisdom of the owl
Fire of a dragon
Flight of a fairy
And from the strength of unicorns.

They say---
"It's not the destination, but the journey."
This one rings true.
At any time
We feel lost
We can visit
our own
Secret Garden---
where we have many helpers.

They are patient
guiding us
Until
we Remember
our power---
and find our way home
like Dorothy did.

More Messages
by Le'Vell Zimmerman

#8

You are experiencing your own level of integrity
at present beloved.

When you change...

Those reflections among your relationships will
as well.

But you first.

Inside, then outside is how it works here in the
hologram.

#333

Maturity

Your projections of judgment, shame, and/or guilt
is "not helping" anybody beloved.

It's actually hurting you, where these lower vibrational
energies and projections are only creating more suffering
for you within your experience.

Your healing is in having the maturity to accept and
respect the free will decisions of others beyond
your own expectations.

The truth of unconditional love cultivated within
through honoring all life and their free will decisions.

The purity of Unconditional Love is beyond the
judgments of right and wrong or good and bad.

Acceptance begins within.

#333

#9

You always have exactly what you need, to do what
you need to, right now.

Not what you "want to do", but what you need to do,
where your higher self is orchestrating the entirety of
this sacred process.

It's only necessary to demonstrate the spiritual maturity
in which to trust yourself beyond what the Ego Mind
feels makes logical sense.

Once again, Love is beyond he limitations of logical
comprehension, where you designed this path as a
manifestation of Infinite Intelligence.

One step at a time beloved, where silence is always
guiding you as to what is necessary right now.

When in doubt, be still.

The silence knows.

#3333

#10

There is absolutely nothing to "agree with" here.

The divine truth within the Heart Space is beyond
the Ego minds need for consensus.

Those souls who resonate with these transmissions
simply acknowledge what is felt within, where those
who don't are sophisticated enough to simply not
pay attention.

To "disagree" and take the time to voice or write that
you don't resonate is in truth you still "giving energy to"
these expressions.
Whatever you give energy to, you create more of in your
experience.
19

This is clearly reflective of the insanity of the Ego Mind identity, where mature souls only give energy or "pay attention" to that which they desire more of within their reality.

This is about you trusting yourself more beloved, where the Heart Space has never been dependent on "proof".

#3333

#11

Consider to your self the "programs of limitation" you still hold onto beloved.

Whatever you are telling yourself about this experience is only truly applicable to those allowing themselves to accept and hold onto such limiting thought forms.

For example; if someone tells you that "these kinds of people are like this...", this is a program you have the choice of accepting or not, where upon acceptance the hologram will create the experiences as proof that this program is real.

The same principle applies to not accepting it, where your holographic experience will reveal to you proof of the exact opposite.

Beloved as the Creator you get to decide the conditions of your present experience, your personal experience will continue to be based on what you continue to emotionally tell yourself about life as Source.

Whatever you allow the voice of Ego to express and continue to entertain about this experience, just know "your right"...

However, the eternal truth is Peace.

Mirage by Cheryl

The way home---

I think about a shortcut---
a way out of this reality.

The only way out
is through it.

When I was pregnant
and it was getting close to my time,
I was terrified of delivery--
but I told myself
the only way out
is through it.

A sleepless night---
the only way out
is through it.

You can't mourn
what you never had---
It's all a mirage--
a hologram.

Friendships, arrangements, deals--
all part of the hologram.

Pantoum by Fiona Marks

Lying here awake thoughts running wild
Revisiting the dark no peace tonight
Sleep dreams more real than stark white day
Dissolving fragments ragged edges blurred

Revisiting the dark no peace tonight
Vivid shadows scare away the moon
Dissolving fragments ragged edges blurred
Unfinished poems swim against the tide

Vivid shadows scare away the moon
Restless heartbeat crashing of the waves
Unfinished poems swim against the tide
Forgotten melody rising from the deep

Restless heartbeat crashing of the waves
Sleepy dreams more real than stark white day
Forgotten melody rising from the deep
Lying here awake thoughts running wild

Things I learned on Maui
by Cheryl

Nothing is permanent.

You can start over---

again, again and again

Only by Cheryl

corruption, greed, and ignorance---

Chem trails--
Prescribed burns--
"Thinning" of forests--

Every night, Gaia
and the land here grieve
the negative energies placed upon her---

She is saturated.
She calls for our help--

In the mourning--
the sun rises--
dissolving the last remnants
of the previous days atrocities--

Only
to begin again.

Camp of Humanity **by Cheryl**

Welcome Home!

What does your tent look like?
Is it square, round or pyramid shaped?
Made of sticks, straw or bricks?

Some say---
Follow Us.
We are leading the Way.
Our camp is better, shinier.

I say---
We are all important--
No one group leads the way--
There are many groups in the Camp of Humanity.

I was told--
You don't understand---
You don't live the way we do.
You are a house dweller.

We may live in different structures
Some on wheels--
In trees--
or even underground--

Lets remember what it means to be human.

compassion, humility, dignity--
allowing , accepting and including--

We are all in the ship together.
This ship called Earth
is accelerating---

Soon,
she will reach the speed of light---
speed of thought---

She has invited us along for the journey.

How will we behave on the trip?
Will we fight with our fellow passengers?

Do we think we deserve a better seat---
First class?

Do we hold grudges,
blame others
for our circumstances---
past, present, future

Do we judge others as unworthy?
It's their own fault
they are where they are.

We each have been given
a 'seat' on this journey---

We can move at any time--
pivot
adjust
grow

Become more than our programming.
Unify.

We are the many
and we are One.

Welcome to the Camp of Humanity.

Humble Conclusion by Eden Sky

I have arrived at the conclusion,
yet again, that the only logical response
to the persistently apparent conundrum
of our human existence, is Art.

In this light,
I stand naked before Creation
I stand raw within Creation

From the cosmology
born of the stars in my soul,
I affirm that
all emanations and expressions
sourced from our hearts
are drops of pure art
that bless
the one
mysterious existence
that we call Life.

And, from my puzzling
human journey to yours,
I offer this:

Make space
to listen
to your soul

She has a message
for you...

She has a song
to lift your heart up
to face the sky within...

She is waiting
to guide you
to free the past
back to the winds

to re-circulate
the stored
time-lines...

She is your bravest ally,
waiting to show you
the blossoming secrets
of how to regenerate yourself,

how to shatter the old,
worn-out shells,
and
invoke
the
New
Ray
of
your
infinite
shine

Art Knows by Cheryl

The yin and yang of our heart---
can be found--

in the buzz of a bee
the stripes of a zebra
and the colors of a sunset.

At---
the end of a rainbow
the point of an arrow
the curve of a circle---

There is an intersection
a special place
where we find
more--
A doorway---
                    passage---
Entry point to a new dimension---
Where energy and mass are all the same---
Some call it-- zero point, the event horizon, the aurora.

They say 'Time is Art'
I say there is no time---
only a place where beauty is waiting
to be found
and become someone's art.
Discovery.

Art is a wise woman.
She already knows.
Waiting for us to find her---
like peace
She is available to all.

Creation by Cheryl

There is a truth---

If you envision something
(the realms of cause) (5D)
You bring it down---
to the field of reality (3D)
it becomes physical (real).

Full by Cheryl

Joy Full
Be U til Full
Great Full

A Message by Cheryl

Every day is a different reality---
Yesterday's events
matter not.
It's all a hologram anyway--

So you don't need to be concerned--
Try to fix anyone--

Tomorrow
we'll all be awash
in an ocean
of sunlight.

Just be kind,
the rest will work itself out.

With a Little Help from My Friends
by Darrel Johannes

My friends understand they stand as one,
are willing to feel what I feel.
They have made peace with their grief, their errors, their angst--
so they have no fear of mine.

My friends know that the idol of absolute personal power is a myth.
This myth has been destroyed by honesty, by the truth of life's
experience .

My friends know there is no real connection without vulnerability--
showing their tender and kind underbelly.
I trust their kindness and safety and they trust mine.

My friends understand that much of what we have been taught, the
cultural norms; do not serve their purpose in life and do not honor
our reality as children of god.

My friends know that there is this something, this voice, this
ancient script that speaks of higher ways, kinder ways, absolute life
giving ways. They listen, honor and trust this voice. That I to, listen,
honor and trust.

My friends are Iconoclasts as am I. We love playing with the
wrecking ball, the one that destroys the patterns and values that
never did honor who we really are. We are escape artists.

My friends know that life is joy, and being heavy is just plain
useless. We choose not to repeat the patterns of despair.

My friends know that my wholeness and joy is their wholeness and
joy, so they see no value in jealousy and envy. This stuff of fallen
Angels poisons the soul and has no place in our hearts.

For my friends can be no other way than---
Mercy, Love and Compassion.

Who are these people I speak of ?

Poetry Eludes Me
by Rita Chambers

Poetry eludes me
like the days themselves,
falling like pages one upon another.

Never time
for remembrance, nor the taste of
rain
falling from the skies.

Lived are the prayers
folded and pressed in layers
and amber dusted sleeves.

A beauteous flurry
petaled once upon a time,
foretold and lifted now.

Revelation now must mark
the poem feathered without end
nor to be set free.

On Turning 80
by Maria Lodes

What is this day—
  what matters it to me
Turning 80
  or not...

Either there is no effect
  —just another year
Or great consequence—
  depending the (E)eye that sees...

In between they coalesce
  —acceptance and resistance
Neither one nor the other
  —Being all That Is...

Feeling the backfire
  from eons ago—
This walk-through life
  full-up with regrets—

Thinking eye recreates
  past memories—
Magnifies them
  —virtual horror stories...

Injustice is karmic backfire
  —a smattering of thoughts
Released in the exhaust
  of misfired cylinders...

Smoothing the fabric
  —hand of love
Tool of the Universe
  restores equanimity...

Neither this nor that
  —No egoic mind
On the Rise
  leaving illusion behind...

I hear them
     calling to me—
Finish this business
     you have come here to do...

There's more
     that needs doing—
Promises to keep
     on the Other Side...

Wake-up Call
     em-brazens me—
Give up this notion
     being some one—

Reeling in
     the past—
My plans
     for the future—

Being
     Contented
Where I'm At—
     Present in the Moment...

33

The Blue Expanse
by Darrel Johannes

From end to end, with the ends ever expanding.
The nature of heaven itself being one of never
ending expansion.

'And of the increase of his kingdom there shall
be no end.'

The fullness being in a way an absence of all
clutter, and things of falsehood, of no real value.

Beyond explanation, the fact being, the beauty
of it and also that it is removed from human
language puts it in a place, where it cannot
be touched by the impurity and limits of our
plane of consciousness.

The yearning for the blue expanse is joy itself.
The journey actually more vital than the destination.
Joy being in the <u>movement </u>towards the thing that
draws.

This blue expanse, one must leave the confines,
the limits of the present reality to experience it.
It does not exist with our logic or because of it,
it lives by a different set of precepts; Love over
judgment and hope over despair.

Its nature is one of momentum and grace, loving
what is and it is on track and on time. It exists for
no particular reason in the way we understand
purpose. It cares about all but will not be brought
down to our problems. It asks and would so love
for us to simply lift up our eyes to the horizon and
embrace the beauty of it. Feel it, and for just a
while, become,
into it.

great egret by the lake
by Michelle Berditschevsky

crickets and frogs have become quiet
geese are flying north

war drums are rolling a beat
that doesn't coincide with our hearts

bugles sound heroic wails
that ring false to our feelings

oaks are turning yellow
summer fruits fall on the ground

I walk by the lake, and there
unexpectedly, is the great egret

anchoring a long moment
of perfect stillness

lone white egret of my solitude
I'll never regret

having wrecked on this reef
as long as I find you

I'm only a visitor
to the continuous song of these waves

asking for just one word
to take back to the human shore

for one moment when the curtain
parts, relentless time

stops, and suddenly I hear
the one living word that carries my heart

above the chatter
in crowded rooms behind closed doors

Returning Home to Soul
by A'Marie B. Thomas-Brown

Light/shadow both illuminate...

Internal signals lead me

on my path to my true self...

the totality of my experience

A Divinely challenged passage...

The Emptying of identity...

The dissolving & evolving...

In the space in between...

The gap between thoughts,

& in breath & outbreath...

The absence of resistance...

The Expansiveness of possibility...

Allowing grace, in this unknown

yet known space...

Of formless dimension...

Where pure Consciousness abides...

Returning Home to Soul.

Home by Cheryl

Death is the door---
sail away--
the Highway to Heaven.

'Halt'
There is a tin man
guarding the door.

Hire the liars---
their story will make you gasp.
It was leaked--
Can we trust it?
Don't believe everything you hear.

Roam the room.
Meet--
Face to Face.
Be the cue.
Dance a jig--loose your wig--
Walk the wag.

Play that funky music--
shake your tail
sail your boat
spread your wings

Enter the art--
Gape, Vibe, Jive.
Vedas.

End your journey
as a hero--
Call off the search.
Always seeking, looking--
Be done---
If it pleases you,
be true to yourself...
Fold up the maps---
We've found our way
Home!

Many thanks to these contributors:

Orasin Orasin

Albert Einstein

Jennifer Hershelman

Darrel Johannes

A'Marie B. Thomas-Brown

Le'Vell Zimmerman

Mercy (Hawkwomyn) Talley

Shambala

Fiona Marks

Eden Sky

Rita Chambers

Jan Dorrell

Maria Lodes and

Michelle Berditschevsky

Author page--

Cheryl Lunar Wind lives in the Mount Shasta area in a little town called Weed. She is a practicer of Mayan cosmology, Lakota ceremony, Star Knowledge and the Universal Laws including the Law of One. Her hobbies are writing poetry, music, dance, drum circles and love for all life; plant, animal and crystal. Cheryl has been a guide and spiritual teacher for many years. Now she shares wisdom and wit through poetry, and has published poetry books; Know Your Way, We Are One, Follow the White Rabbit, Love Your Light, LIFE: Shared thru Poetry, Come to Mount Shasta: Sacred Path Poetry, We Are Light, Finding Our Way Home, and co-authored We Are Forever: Awaken With Poetry.

Testimonials---

"Cheryl's poetry is very inspiring--particularly the way she compares life with the forces of nature. There is a special element in her poems that opens my heart and fills my soul with divine possiblities."
Giovanna Taormina, Co-Founder, One Circle Foundation

"Cheryl's poems have helped me to uncover and honor my own hidden memories. The beauty of her spirit is evident in each tender, insightful passage."
Marguerite Lorimer, www.earthalive.com

"A rare collection filled with raw, courageous honesty. Thought provoking words that will stop you in your tracks."
Snow Thorner, ED Open Sky Gallery, Montague, California

"When wisdom, guidance, confirming comfort, ect. arrives to us humans--from beings with the perspective of other realms--it is a divine gift. Especially in the form of what we call poetry, and through a being with no agenda; Cheryl Lunar Wind simply shares what source gives her!"
--Dragon Love (Thomas) Budde

www.ingramcontent.com/pod-product-compliance
Lightning Source LLC
Chambersburg PA
CBHW060632030426
42337CB00018B/3317